PUFFIN B

Editor: Kaye

GEORG

George was a very un-ordinary hopped into the Weaver househo proved to be a very un-ordinary day. For George wore glasses, he could talk, and he was good at arithmetic, which particularly pleased Milly and Tommy. He was very helpful to Mrs Weaver, too, while Milly and Tommy were at school; only their father remained sceptical and refused to believe in George. In fact he forbade Milly and Tommy to talk about him. How could they make their father understand? It wasn't until they were just about to set off on their summer holiday that Mr Weaver found George's note . . .

Agnes Sligh Turnbull

George

illustrated by

Trina Schart Hyman

Puffin Books

in association with Collins

Puffin Books: a Division of Penguin Books Ltd,
Harmondsworth, Middlesex, England
Penguin Books Australia Ltd, Ringwood, Victoria, Australia

—

First published in the U.S.A. 1965
First published in Great Britain by Collins 1967
Published in Puffin Books 1970
Reprinted 1971, 1974

—

—

Made and printed in Great Britain by
Hazell Watson & Viney Ltd,
Aylesbury, Bucks
Set in Linotype Pilgrim

To my grandson

JIMMY

with my love

I

Mrs Weaver had woken up that morning with a bad headache. She managed to get down to the kitchen in her dressing gown and prepare breakfast for Mr Weaver, who always had to catch a train for the city, and for Milly and Tommy who had to be at school by a quarter to nine. When they were all gone she made some peanut butter and jelly sandwiches which she wrapped in wax paper and left on the table for the children's lunch in case she wasn't able to come downstairs again. She knew Milly could get the milk out of the refrigerator and the biscuits from the tin. Milly was eight and very capable. Tommy was six and had to be watched in case he made his whole lunch on biscuits and forgot his sandwiches. When she had finished her work she went slowly upstairs and lay down again in bed. Her head hurt her very much.

For a while the house was perfectly quiet, then she

began to hear something. It seemed like soft little velvet pat-pats on the stairs. At first she thought it was the throbbing in her head, then the small strange sounds grew a bit louder in the upper hall and stopped. Very slowly she opened her eyes. There in the doorway sat a brown rabbit. It appeared to be like any other good-sized rabbit she had ever seen except that this one wore glasses. He looked back at her and bowed slightly.

'Name is George,' he said. 'George H. Since everyone asks what the *H* stands for I'll tell you right away. Stands for Hare. My grandfather was a Belgian Hare. Very fine family.'

'How did you get in?' Mrs Weaver asked faintly.

'Kitchen window. Tommy left it open. As usual.'

'You know Tommy?'

'Of course. I've spent a good deal of time in your garden.'

Mrs Weaver's eyes opened wider. 'Then it's you who has been eating my young lettuce?'

'Now, now!' said George, adjusting his glasses since the twitching of his nose made them slide down a little. 'I hoped that matter wouldn't come up. I admit I may have nibbled, but only the edges. To change the subject, what is the matter with you?'

'A headache,' she moaned. 'It's very severe!'

'Oh, if that's all, I can cure it. Don't be startled. I'm coming up on the bed.'

With one big leap he settled himself close to Mrs Weaver.

'If you'll excuse my back,' he said, 'I'll sit here while you stroke me, ears to tail. You'll soon find you are growing sleepy. When you wake up your headache will be gone. Go ahead. Try it!'

Mrs Weaver slowly put out her hand and began to move it over George's fur. She had never felt anything so deliciously soft in her life. Back and forth, back and forth went her hand and more and more she began to feel drowsy. At last, as George had predicted, she fell asleep. He stayed there for a long time and then when he felt it must be nearly time for the children to be back for lunch he hopped to the floor and very quietly pat-patted his way downstairs and into the big kitchen. He saw the sandwiches wrapped and ready, and then jumped up in one of the chairs and waited.

When Milly and Tommy came in, I'm sorry to say, they were quarrelling.

'You stop bossing me!' Tommy shouted. 'Just because you're older you can't tell me what to do.'

'I can so!' Milly shouted back. 'And you'd better wait for me the next time, the way Mother told you to. If you don't I'll . . .'

She had gripped a clump of Tommy's hair when George spoke up in his small but very clear voice.

'That's enough,' he said. 'I'm really surprised at you both.'

Milly and Tommy saw him then for the first time, their eyes growing larger and larger. Then they looked at each other as though to say, 'Do you see and hear what I do?'

George adjusted his glasses.

'Would you let any other little girl pull your brother's hair, Milly?' he asked.

'N-no,' she said, 'I wouldn't.'

'Well then. If you feel like that about it, isn't it rather silly for you to do it yourself?'

'I . . . I suppose so,' said Milly, hanging her head.

'And you, Tommy. There's a good reason why you should wait to walk home with Milly, isn't there?'

'Y-yes,' Tommy admitted.

'I should say so. Crossing streets nowadays has to be a careful business. Friend of mine got killed last week by not watching out. Of course a dog was chasing him. Well, I think we have things settled, then, so run along and wash your hands. Girls first,' he added.

When the children were seated at the table they kept

looking at their visitor and then at each other in a very puzzled way.

'Should have introduced myself,' the guest said. 'Name is George. George H. Rabbit. *H* stands for Hare. My grandfather was a Belgian Hare. Very handsome. Long ears and all that. It's why I wear glasses,' he added.

'Not to help your eyes?' Milly asked in surprise.

'Not a bit. Eyes are fine. But my grandfather wore

them, so I do, too. Upon occasion. Adds to my appearance I think.'

The children looked at each other again and then back to George.

'Would you care for some lunch?' Milly asked politely. 'We never eat quite all our sandwiches.'

'Thank you,' said George. 'Just a modicum, please. That means a little. Always learn new words when you can. A bit of sandwich would be a pleasant change. I usually eat only young *greens*.'

Both children said '*Oh!*' at once in a very meaningful tone. George seemed to stiffen.

'I explained about that to your mother. We won't bring it up again. How did school go this morning?'

Milly and Tommy both sighed.

'My Arithmetic wasn't right.'

'Neither was mine,' said Tommy.

'Dear me!' George scratched one ear delicately. 'When do you do your homework?'

'Well, it's like this,' Milly explained. 'We can watch television before dinner, but after we eat we have to do our chores, then our homework, and then go to bed. It's all very boring.'

'I don't know,' said George. 'That seems reasonable to me, as long as you can see television *before* dinner. Where do you do your studying?'

'Right here. On the kitchen table. We like it this way, for we have room to spread out our papers,' Tommy said.

'Good!' George replied. 'Tonight I'll help you. Arith-

metic is my best subject. My grandfather taught me. He was a wonder with numbers. O.K.?'

'You really mean it?' Milly said breathlessly.

'I've just said so,' George answered. He raised a paw to his head. 'Honour of a rabbit!' he pronounced solemnly.

'Oh, that will be wonderful! We'd better go now and speak to Mother. She told us she mightn't be down to lunch.' Milly had risen from her chair.

'No,' said George. 'She's asleep. Don't disturb her. She'll be down here when you get back from school, I know.'

'Will you be here then, too?' Tommy asked eagerly.

‘I’m not sure just what my plans for the afternoon will be,’ George said. ‘But I’ll keep my promise for the evening. Run along now.’

The children had stopped looking surprised. They both waved goodbye to him as though to a dear friend.

George finished his bit of sandwich and biscuit, and then made a tour of the kitchen and pantry. He finally discovered a cosy little spot in the latter, behind the clothes drier and next to the broom cupboard. Here, no one could see him.

‘Location is perfect,’ George said to himself. He hopped in, settled his head upon his paws and went fast asleep.

When Milly and Tommy came back from school they rushed through the kitchen calling, 'George! George! Where are you? *George!*'

But George remained quiet in his hiding place. He heard them talking excitedly to their mother, and then at last go out with her in the car to meet their father's train. It was Mr Weaver whom George was anxious about. He hardly knew whether to introduce himself, or not. Men were different.

When the station wagon rolled again along the drive, the family all came in the back way. Milly was talking excitedly.

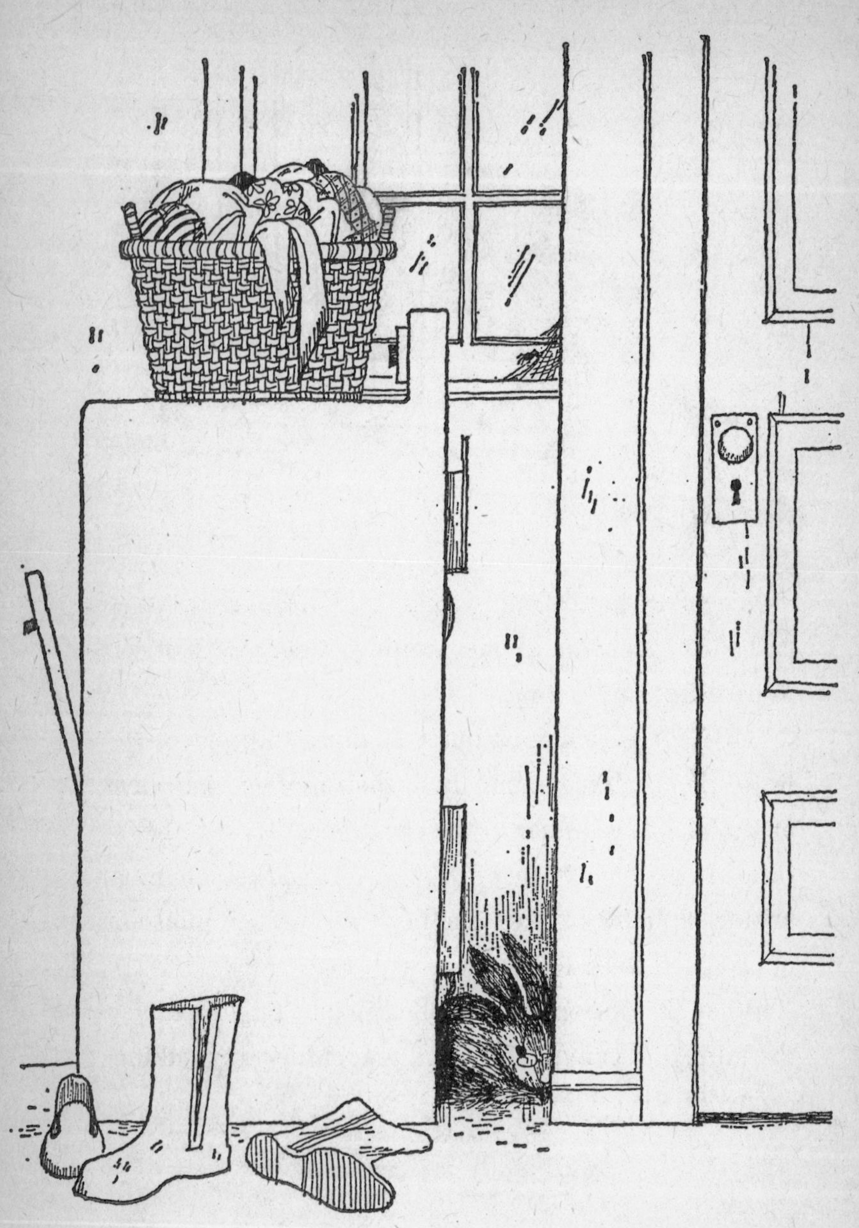

'But Father, he was *here*. Really, truly! He ate lunch with us. And he can *talk*. He even uses big words.'

'And he wears *glasses*!' Tommy added.

'And his name's George!'

'Well! Well!' Mr Weaver said. 'Now, isn't that interesting!'

'But Mother saw him, too. Didn't you, Mother?'

George turned his head in order to hear her answer more clearly.

'I either saw him or I *dreamed* him,' Mrs Weaver said.

'Oh, Father, you don't believe us,' Milly cried. 'You

look just the way you did the day we saw the fairy in the apple tree!'

'And Mother saw something then, too. She said so,' Tommy put in earnestly.

And then George heard their father laugh. It was a nice laugh, very tender. He couldn't be sure but he had the feeling somehow that Mr Weaver was kissing Mrs Weaver.

'I know now,' he was saying,' why our children can see fairies and rabbits who wear glasses! Well, I'm going to take a little rest. This was a hard day in the office. And if George comes in,' he called back, still laughing, but in a different way, 'tell him I'll be pleased to see him.'

'That settles it,' George said grimly to himself. 'I don't intend to meet him. Ever. So there!'

From Milly's description at lunch he could tell just what was happening. The children were watching television while their mother prepared the dinner. Nice smells came from the stove but George would have exchanged all the food there for some lettuce leaves and carrot tops if he had the choice. He could hear the voices from the dining room while dinner was in progress and then the children moving about at their

chores. Tommy, apparently, cleared the table and emptied the kitchen waste bucket; Milly wiped the dishes. When all was finished Mrs Weaver spoke.

'Now children, start your homework. And please try very hard to do it properly. I hope your next month's report cards will be better than the last time. I'm going into the living room now with Father and you can watch the clock, Tommy. At eight sharp, you must be off to bed. Then Milly at eight-thirty.'

George came out of his nook very softly for he didn't want anyone to know his hiding place. As he entered

the kitchen Milly was saying, almost in tears, 'But he *promised*!'

'And here I am,' said George briskly, jumping up on a chair between them. 'Now, let's begin. What do you have to do, Tommy?'

The children were so happy to see him that for a few moments they couldn't speak. They just stroked his soft back, turn about, and Milly even placed a little kiss between his ears. He shook his head a bit after this for he wasn't sure he liked being kissed. The stroking was all right. And of course he was happy that the children were fond of him.

'Well, Tommy?' he repeated.

'I have to do the *four times* table perfect. I missed it today.'

'And I have some *dreadful* examples in division and

multiplication both! I'll never get them right!' Milly groaned.

'Of course you will. Just buckle down to it. *Concentrate*. That means make your mind work hard. I'll hear Tommy's tables while you do your problems.'

Tommy always made a mistake when he got to four times nine. Each time he said *thirty-four*. George puckered up his eyes as though thinking.

'I'll tell you!' he said. 'The right answer rhymes with *sticks*. Now, you remember that and try it again. From the beginning.'

Tommy repeated slowly, and finally said, 'Four times nine is – sticks – *thirty-six*!'

'Fine!' said George. 'Now say it all over twice and I think you'll have it!'

When Tommy was finished and very pleased indeed with himself, George turned to Milly's paper and scanned it carefully.

'It is my considered opinion,' he said at last, 'that according to my grandfather's teaching, these problems are all right!'

Milly clapped her hands. 'If I get a hundred on this tomorrow, I'll be *so* happy! You know, George, I really worked hard tonight. Usually I keep getting up to call

one of my friends on the phone, or look at the clock or chatter to Tommy. It's so much easier when you are beside us. Will you be here each night?'

'For a while,' said George. 'I like it here. Nice house. Nice family. Eight o'clock, Tommy. You'd better scamper.'

'Couldn't you come up, when we're in bed? *Please*, George!' Tommy was almost breathless, he was so eager.

'Well, well, hurry along. We'll see.'

Tommy didn't argue or complain or delay as he usually did. He put up his book, said goodnight to his father and fairly ran up the stairs. Later when Milly was in the living room and Mrs Weaver had heard Tommy's prayers, kissed him and come down again, George quietly pat-patted up. He heard Tommy's low *hoo-hoo* so he knew which room to go into. Once there he jumped on the bed and snuggled close to Tommy. The little boy put his arms around his new friend and drew a long breath.

'You're so soft . . . and comfortable, George. I really love you!' And in a very few minutes he was fast asleep.

George waited a while, then got down and sat under

the bed. He heard Milly come up and move around in the next room. He heard Mrs Weaver come later and say goodnight, then all was quiet. He hopped into Milly's room and leaped up beside her. Milly drew him close to her and kissed him again between his ears. He didn't mind so much this time. In fact he rather liked it.

'Please stay on with us, George,' she begged. 'It's so wonderful having a rabbit like you in the family.'

She stroked his fur gently for a little while and then she, too, fell asleep.

As George was going downstairs he overheard the children's parents talking in the living room.

'It was amazing,' Mrs Weaver said, 'how quickly Tommy and Milly went to bed tonight! I've been having a lot of trouble with them lately. They keep fussing and wanting drinks of water and all sorts of things.'

'Oh, it's just a phase they've been going through,' Mr Weaver said very wisely, 'and have got over it now. Besides they probably were tired tonight.'

George sniggered to himself. 'A lot he knows about it!' he thought.

Once back in the kitchen he looked around him. He planned to stay outside during the night and wanted a place to hide his glasses. It wasn't safe to wear them in the garden. He had lost them once in a flower bed and

it had taken him most of a day to find them. Now he noticed the big blue breadbox on the end of the counter, which sat partly in front of the windowsill. This might just do! He jumped up and looked behind it. Anything on the sill behind the box would be completely hidden. George carefully took off his glasses, folded them and laid them on the sill. Then he got down and went to the back door. He knew it didn't fasten well for Tommy was always leaving it unlatched. He scratched now with one paw, then nudged it with his nose. At last it opened and he hopped out into the lovely, soft spring darkness.

2

As the weeks went on, George settled himself comfortably into the Weaver household. He appeared at the kitchen door each morning after Mr Weaver had left, and while the children were finishing their breakfast. He hopped around the house later with Mrs Weaver while she was doing her work, then ate lunch with Milly and Tommy, after which he retired behind the clothes drier and slept all afternoon. But though there were always many calls of '*George! George!* Where are you?' when the children got home from school at three-thirty George never left his hiding place until time for the homework after dinner.

One evening when the Arithmetic was nearly done – and it was going better all the time, by the way – Milly spoke very seriously.

'George,' she said, 'you know how much we love you, but it does worry us that you never come in when Father is here. He's really very nice, you know.'

'Indeed,' said George, 'a most delightful gentleman.'

'Then *why* . . . ?' pursued Milly.

'Well, I'll tell you. Once I even went so far as to peep around the living room when you were all there. You and Tommy were talking to your father about me. And he said . . .'

Here George stopped and his nose twitched violently.

'He said, "If you and Tommy want to believe that there is a rabbit here which talks and wears glasses you can do so. But please don't ask *me* to believe it!"'

Milly sighed heavily.

'And that wasn't all,' George went on. 'He added that he didn't think you children should imagine such ridiculous things either.'

'I remember,' Milly said sadly. 'George, if he just once could *see* you . . .'

'But that's the point,' George said. 'I don't think he could see me if I sat right in front of him. No, the plain fact is that your father and I are not *congenial*.'

'What's that?' Tommy asked quickly.

'To be congenial with anyone means you get on well with him. Now, remember that word, Tommy. You should try every day to add to your vocabulary.'

'What's vo-cab-u-lary?' Tommy persisted.

'It's the number of words you can use. Properly. Well now, let's go ahead with the Arithmetic.'

But Milly soon looked up from her problems. 'George, you do get on well with Mother, don't you?'

'Oh, yes!' said George. 'I get on famously with her. She's about the nicest woman I've ever met.'

So with this the children had to be content.

As a matter of fact George felt so much at home with Mrs Weaver that he even offered advice sometimes. One morning when she was tidying the linen cupboard he spoke, behind her.

'Would you mind if I made a suggestion?'

'Why, not at all,' said Mrs Weaver, examining a sheet to see if the hem needed mending. 'What would you like to say?'

'It's in connexion with the children's manners, which in the main are very good, I must admit,' he added. 'Still there are one or two little matters in which they could improve.'

'Such as what?' Mrs Weaver asked, as she began re-arranging the pile of pillow slips.

'Well,' said George, 'I notice that both Milly and Tommy are inclined to go through a door ahead of you. They should wait, of course, and let you or any older person go first.'

'I have been a bit careless about that, I'm afraid,' Mrs Weaver admitted. 'We often come in from the car in a rush and they're into the house before I realize it. I'll watch out for that from now on.'

'My grandfather always said that if children didn't have good manners on weekdays they wouldn't have on Sundays. I suppose you know what he meant.'

Mrs Weaver laughed. 'If they didn't have beautiful manners at home they wouldn't have elsewhere. Is that it?'

'Right,' said George. 'I was thinking, too, that

Tommy is old enough now to seat you in your chair in the dining room at dinner. I know he doesn't yet, for I asked him. If he learns to do it now he will feel manly and important and perform the courtesy naturally as he gets older. Just my opinion,' he added, adjusting his glasses nervously, for above all things he didn't want to offend Mrs Weaver.

She paused now. 'I believe,' she said, 'that I'd better order some new bath towels. But as to seating me at the table, that would be rather nice for Tommy to do. I'll speak to his father about it.'

George started to hop away, then turned.

'Just one other little thing,' he said hesitantly.

'I'd better order a few new linen towels too,' Mrs Weaver was murmuring. 'A number of these are getting thin. Oh, what did you want to say, George?'

'I've noticed lately that Tommy is getting the habit of saying "*Pardon*", when he doesn't hear the first time. That is not correct. One should say "*Excuse me*" or "*I beg your pardon*", as ... as of course you know. My grandfather was always very particular about this. I do hope you don't mind my mentioning it!'

'Oh, not at all,' Mrs Weaver reassured him. 'I'll watch that, and thank you. It's been quite an interesting conversation, George, although,' she went on with her chuckling laugh, 'I'm never sure whether I'm talking to myself or to you!'

But George was quite content and set himself to watch for the results of his suggestions. The first came that very evening as he peered from behind the clothes drier. Milly and Tommy rushed pell-mell through the back door in front of their mother and then she brought them back to wait until she had entered first.

'Good!' George muttered. 'Very good! Hope she keeps it up. They'll soon learn.'

Some nights later, his ears raised and listening sharply, he could tell that something unusual was going on as the family sat down to dinner. Later he heard all about it from Tommy, who was puffed up with pride like a pigeon.

'Do you know what I did this evening, George?'

'Couldn't guess.'

'I seated my mother at dinner!'

'Well! Well!'

'My father says it's time I learned the manners of a gentleman!'

'Quite so!'

'And my father says if we don't have beautiful manners every day at home . . .'

'We won't have them when we're out visiting,' Milly finished.

'Fancy that!' said George drily. 'Your father must be a remarkable man.'

'Oh, he is!' Milly agreed. 'And so nice in every way except one. Do you know, George, we have trouble about you with other people too?'

'How so?'

'Well, we've stopped talking to the other children

for they all say you aren't *real*. And then just today my teacher asked me how my Arithmetic has improved so wonderfully and I said it was all because of *George* and she asked me who George was so I told her you were a rabbit and that your grandfather was a Belgian Hare and had taught you, and she didn't like it. She said it wasn't polite for me to joke with her in that way and she wouldn't let me explain that I *wasn't* joking.'

George said nothing. As a matter of fact his heart felt very heavy. Then Milly began to stroke his soft fur, and gently put a kiss between his ears.

'But *we* know you're real, George, and we love you so, don't we, Tommy?'

'You just bet we do!' said Tommy.

George drew a long breath. 'Then that's quite enough for me,' he said. 'Let's get on with the Arithmetic.'

One Friday afternoon George roused from his nap as Milly and Tommy raced into the kitchen shouting, 'Mother! Mother! George! George! George!' at the top of their voices. Their mother came at once.

'Whatever is it?' she asked.

'We each got an *A* in Arithmetic on our report cards!' Milly sang out.

'Each of us! The two of us! Milly and me both!' Tommy repeated.

'Milly and *I*,' their mother corrected. 'Why, I'm so surprised and happy I don't know what to do! This calls for a celebration. What do you say to ice cream and cake for dessert? Let me see the cards. Oh! Oh! I'm so terribly proud of you and just wait till your father hears about this! Here's a kiss for each of you!'

'We knew you'd be pleased,' Milly said, 'didn't we, Tommy?'

'You bet!' said Tommy.

'Oh, I've an idea!' their mother went on. 'If there's a nice Walt Disney picture anywhere near, perhaps we could all go tonight! Wouldn't that be wonderful?'

The telephone rang just then and she hurried into the study to answer it. Milly and Tommy moved nearer the kitchen door which was fine for George, because he could hear better.

'This is going to be awful,' Milly said almost in tears. 'Just when we were so happy, too. How can we leave George out of *everything*?'

'I don't think we ought to go to the pictures tonight,' said Tommy stoutly. 'He might even just come in when nobody's here.'

'We'll ask if we can't go tomorrow night, instead. Maybe they'll let us.'

'If they don't have a 'gagement themselves,' Tommy said.

'We can say we want to put our puzzles together on the kitchen table after dinner the way we did last week.'

'And save some dessert for George, somehow. Oh dear, it's so com ... com ... *com*pilated,' lamented Tommy.

'Complicated, you goose. You know, Tommy, what I've a notion to do?'

'What?'

'I think I'll tell Mother all about it. I do believe she would understand.'

'What would I understand?' Mrs Weaver asked as she came back into the kitchen.

Milly hesitated and then began to speak very fast.

'Well, you see, Mother, it was George that helped us get our *A*s in Arithmetic and we just can't have all the celebration without him, now can we? We thought maybe we could go to the pictures tomorrow night and this evening we could visit with him like we always do.'

'And maybe save him some ice cream and cake,' Tommy put in eagerly.

George was listening so hard his ears were standing straight up except for a nervous wiggle now and then. It seemed to him a long time before Mrs Weaver spoke and then it was in a sort of far-away voice.

'When I was a little girl,' she said, 'I had a pet that no one could see but me. He was a little tiny tiger and his name was Tinkey. I just found him in my room one day when I was sick with measles.'

'Did he get into bed with you?' Tommy asked.

'Oh, yes. And he was so soft and cuddly. When I got well he went everywhere with me. I didn't have a brother or sister, you know, so it was great company for me to have Tinkey. He had the loveliest stripes on

his nose,' she added dreamily. 'He always sat beside me at the table and I tried to feed him little bits of meat, but the dog always got them first.' She laughed then, though George couldn't understand why.

'Did you have Tinkey a long time, Mother?' Milly asked.

'Quite a while. As long as I needed him. Now, let's make plans for tonight. Why couldn't you and Tommy eat a smaller portion of ice cream and cake at the table, then I'll leave some in the refrigerator for you to have later on. With George. And as to the pictures, we can go tomorrow night just as well. I found out there is a good one you'll enjoy.'

There were shouts of pleasure from the children and then Mrs Weaver added as she apparently was leaving the kitchen, 'And please tell George how much I appreciate his helping you with your Arithmetic!'

George scratched one ear delicately. 'Delightful woman, Mrs Weaver, absolutely delightful!' he murmured to himself. 'I should like to have met her friend Tinkey. He evidently was quite tame for a tiger. Nice little chap from what she said.'

Dinner that evening was very happy and hilarious.

The sounds came clearly out to George in his hiding place. The report cards had evidently been placed beside their father's plate and his remarks were most enthusiastic.

'What a change from last month!' he said. 'What an improvement! I always told you that if you just tried a little harder with your homework you could bring your marks up . . . Oh, I am very pleased!'

George listened hard to hear his own name mentioned, but it was not. He put his nose down between his paws and breathed a long sigh.

'Maybe it's just as well,' he thought. 'Mr Weaver simply wouldn't understand.'

After their evening chores were done Milly and Tommy spread their puzzles out on the kitchen table, set George's chair between theirs and laid the report cards open in front of it. George arrived as usual when they weren't looking, and was greeted excitedly. He adjusted his glasses, looked carefully at the cards and acted as though he had not heard the great news before.

'An *A* for Milly! And an *A* for Tommy! In *Arithmetic*! Why this is most wonderful! I am indeed *gratified*!'

'What does that mean?' Tommy asked quickly.

'Pleased,' said George. 'Very much pleased. Now you'll both have to work hard this next month too, won't you?'

'If you'll help us,' said Milly.

'You'll be here, won't you, George?'

'I hope to be,' he said.

'And now,' Milly began, smiling, 'we're having a little party. Wait till you see!'

She brought out three pretty plates and then the ice cream and cake. 'It's specially for you, George. You know why.'

George might at another time have preferred some lacy carrot tops but naturally he never thought of that now, but nibbled away at the cake and did fairly well with the ice cream, too, though Milly and Tommy had to finish both for him in the end.

'Now, let's get to the puzzles,' he said.

The children were trying to fit the states of the United States into their proper places within a framework. George put his glasses farther up on his nose and watched carefully. Milly and Tommy were both very clever at puzzles and had done this one before but even so, Tommy, who went more by the shape of the pieces than by the letter, often became confused and was ready to give up. When this happened George raised a paw and nudged the proper bit of painted wood toward his hand.

'Oh, *there* it is!' Tommy would exclaim. 'How did you ever know that, George?'

'My grandfather taught me Geography too,' George replied. 'He said that even though I never went far beyond my own hedgerow it was well to know what a great and beautiful country I lived in. Here,' he went on, 'this big piece goes in next.'

'That's Texas,' said Milly, rather proud of her knowledge.

'Of course,' George replied. 'I was just about to say that.'

When bedtime came the children agreed it had been a lovely evening but they didn't want it to end. 'When you come up to see us after Mother has said goodnight,

couldn't you stay a little longer than usual, George, 'cause this is a special evening?' Tommy begged.

'And tell us stories about your grandfather?' Milly added.

George's nose twitched quietly for a second before he answered. Then he said, 'I think I can do that, because you both got such good marks and also because ...' Here he paused and Milly and Tommy decided next day that he actually sounded as though he were a little choked up. 'And because,' he went on, 'you planned the party *for me*!'

3

It was on the last day of school that the accident nearly happened. There was only a half-day session, so Milly and Tommy came home triumphantly at lunch time.

'No more school,' they kept shouting. 'No more school till next autumn! Hurray! Hurray!'

They could hardly settle down for lunch, but finally quietened enough to plan what they would do that afternoon. Milly had been invited to spend it with one of her friends up the street. Tommy had a new red ball which had just come from his uncle in yesterday's post.

'I've hardly had time to try it out yet and I'm so very pleased with it. I think I'll just stay in the garden and play with it. If George will come too,' he added hopefully.

'I was expecting to spend the afternoon in the garden,' George replied. 'And it's a very beautiful ball. How did your uncle come to send it to you when it isn't your birthday?'

'Because I'm his namesake, that's why. He's always sending me things.'

'I wish I'd been named for somebody *living*,' Milly said, 'so I'd get presents. I was named for my great-grandmother, so you can see what chance I have. Who were you named for, George?'

'My grandfather. And very proud I am of it. I think, Milly, you should just be satisfied to have a fine name without wanting anything more.'

'Oh, I hope so,' Milly sighed, 'but I do like presents too. Besides, *nobody* else I know of is named *Millicent*.'

'That's good,' said George. 'That makes you unique.'

Tommy pounced at once. 'What does that mean?'

'Unique? Oh, different in a very nice, special way. Well, what about going outside now?'

'We're all ready,' the children said, but George hesitated.

'There is something I must do first,' he almost whispered, 'but it is a secret, in a way.'

He hopped on a chair and from there to the counter, then took off his glasses, folded them carefully and placed them behind the breadbox. Milly and Tommy were entranced.

'Oh, *what* a nice hiding place for them! They'll always be safe there,' Milly exclaimed.

'And you'll never mention it to anyone?' George asked.

'Never, never, *never*!' chorused the children.

'All right then, let's go on.'

Milly took her best doll with her and went on up the street to her friend's. Tommy began to bounce his ball against the garage and against the house while George sat quietly watching him. After a time Tommy grew tired and sat down on the grass beside him.

'Would you do me a great favour?' George asked.

'Of course. What is it?'

'Well,' said George in some embarrassment, 'since I've been staying here I haven't felt I should eat much from the garden. *You* understand. But I wondered if you would pick me a few bits of carrot tops and some of the newest lettuce. It will be quite all right if you do it, you know.'

Tommy was on his feet in a moment. He nipped off some carrot leaves and a nice handful of young lettuce and put them carefully down in front of George.

'I thank you,' he said. 'This is a real treat for me. Just as ice cream is to you!'

'Really?' said Tommy. He picked some more carrot tops and chewed them up manfully. When he managed to swallow them he made a very funny face. 'I *still* like ice cream better, George.'

The lovely June afternoon wore on to four o'clock, then Tommy had a new idea. 'Let's go to the front garden,' he suggested. 'It's shady there and I can try to hit the maple tree with my ball.'

They went round the house, Tommy bouncing the ball as he went while George hopped along beside him. The big maple tree stood near the drive so George sat down at the edge of the lawn where he would have a good view of the play.

'This is going to be fun,' Tommy called out. 'The tree will be the fort and I'm going to bang, bang away at it, and pretend I knock it down! Just watch me!'

It really was rather exciting, for Tommy grew quite skilful in hitting the tree. He threw the ball from one point and then from another, shouting all the time as though he were a soldier trying to take a fortress. All at

once the ball bounced hard from the tree to the pavement and then rolled into the street. In one second Tommy had run after it, not looking to left or right, not seeing the car almost upon him. Then the sound came. A terrible, moaning shriek. Tommy heard, looked up, flung himself out of the street, falling to the pavement beside George who sat there quivering. The car went over the spot where Tommy had just been and came to a stop with grinding brakes just beyond, as the man driving it leaned out of the window and yelled at Tommy. Tommy didn't even hear him. He was shaking all over as he clasped George to his breast.

'Did you make that awful c-cry?' he asked.

'Yes,' George whispered.

'If you hadn't I wouldn't have looked up and seen the car and it would have h-hit me and I might have been k-killed,' Tommy sobbed.

Mrs Weaver came running from the house. 'Oh, Tommy! Oh, darling, are you hurt?'

George quietly hopped back to the garden as he saw Tommy safe in his mother's arms.

'A close squeak,' he kept saying to himself. 'A mighty close squeak. Glad I was there.'

When Mr Weaver got home that night he heard all about it in three different versions. Milly had seen all from the pavement farther up, had tried to call but was too far away.

'Then I saw George on the edge of the pavement,' she

was saying excitedly when her father stopped her.

'Just what, giving no name to it, did you see?' he asked.

'Why, I saw a brown rabbit. It was G—'

'Now Tommy,' their father broke in, 'you tell me all that happened.'

'Well, you see I'd been playing with my new ball and it hit the tree and bounced into the street and I ran out and then George cried and I heard him and got back *just in time*, Father!'

'Thank God! Thank God you did!' Mr Weaver said, and his voice seemed to break as he spoke.

'I was in the living room when I heard the . . . the sound. I've never heard anything like it in my life,' Mrs Weaver put in and her voice trembled too.

'I'm sure you never did,' Mr Weaver said.

'Then you do believe all about it?' Milly said eagerly.

'I certainly believe that a brown rabbit on the edge of the street made the sound that saved Tommy. Oh, my little son!' he added, his voice still not steady. 'That was too close, too close.'

'But you really believe it, Father,' Milly said again.

'Oh yes, I really do,' he replied.

George, behind the clothes drier, snuffed with satisfaction.

'Well now,' he whispered to himself, 'that's something like it! I guess I've really got through to him at last.'

But before dinner when Milly and Tommy were watching TV George heard Mr and Mrs Weaver talking together in the kitchen.

'I was glad you believed about the strange crying, for you know I really heard it.'

'Yes,' he said. 'I heard the same thing once myself. We were hunting and one of the dogs chased a rabbit.

We didn't think of calling it off till we saw it just ready to overtake the bunny. Then the poor thing squatted down as though it knew there was no more use trying to run and gave this heartrending cry. Never heard anything like it before or since.'

'It's sort of like a child in distress and yet different.'

'Yes. One of the other men explained about it that night and I've read of it since. As a rule a rabbit doesn't make a sound. Seems as if it can't. But when it is in terrible danger and feels there is no escape it makes this distress call. Well, I know exactly what happened this afternoon.'

'You do?'

'Why yes, of course. A brown rabbit from one of the

gardens here was just ready to cross the street in front of our house when it saw the car bearing down on it, was terrified and cried out. That's the way it must have been.'

'I wonder,' said Mrs Weaver softly and then George did not hear anything more.

That evening when he was visiting with Tommy in bed, the little boy hugged him close.

'Oh George, I want to thank you for saving my life. I do so want to give you a present. Couldn't you tell me something you would like and I can save up till I have enough money to buy it. Couldn't you, George?'

'There is a present I would like very much.'

'Oh, what is it? No matter how 'spensive it is, I'll get it for you. You'll just see!'

'This present doesn't cost money. What I want you to give me is a *promise*.'

'A promise?'

'Yes. I want you to promise me that you will never, *never* go into a street without stopping first and looking to the left and then to the right. Will you promise me that?'

'I will,' said Tommy.

'Raise your right hand,' said George.

Tommy raised his right hand.

'Honour of a *gentleman?*' asked George.

'Honour of a gentleman,' repeated Tommy slowly and very solemnly indeed.

'That's my present, then,' said George. 'The best one you could give me!'

4

It was nearing the middle of July when George became aware of a certain excitement in the family. The dinner conversation, as he listened to it, was filled with the words *holiday* and *Canada*. Mr Weaver came home from work one afternoon carrying strange poles he said were fishing rods, a long one for himself and a shorter one for Tommy, which news caused Tommy to jump up and down on the kitchen floor and shout so loud he had to be asked to be a little quieter.

Milly, too, had a surprise. A package, ordered by her mother, came from a New York store. It contained what they called a *bathing suit*, though when it was tried on, George thought there was very little of it for a *suit*. Milly was delighted, however, Both she and Tommy were taken shopping often to the town stores to buy what were called *camp clothes*.

George was feeling terribly out of it, but was too proud to ask the children what it was all about. They usually played in the garden under the apple tree now after dinner instead of sitting at the kitchen table as they had done for homework or puzzles. But sometimes George was left alone.

One evening when they were all together, Milly said suddenly, 'I think the trip itself is one of the nicest parts of the holiday.'

'What trip?' George asked a trifle sulkily.

'Why, the trip up to Canada, of course. To our camp. Surely you know we're all going on the first of August!'

'I know nothing,' said George with great dignity. 'I repeat, *nothing*.'

'Oh dear, oh *dear*!' Milly cried. 'Tommy, is it possible we haven't told George before this?'

'Not only possible,' said George very coldly, 'but true.'

'It's because we've been so excited, I expect,' Tommy

said, 'and going shopping and getting ready and everything. Oh, I *am* sorry!'

'So am I,' said Milly. 'Will you forgive us, George, if we tell you about it now? I'll start because I'm the oldest and Tommy can interrupt whenever he wants to. Well, first of all on our holiday we get the station wagon all loaded and then we drive away up to Canada and ...'

'What is *Canada?*' George asked.

'Why, it's a big country just north of the United States and it takes us two days to get there!'

'And we have a house right on a lake,' Tommy said. 'But it's not a bit like our house here. It's called a *cabin* and it doesn't have paper on the walls or anything. Just brown logs inside and outside, and Milly and I have bunk beds ...'

'One on top of the other,' Milly broke in, 'and we can swim in the lake and go out in the boat ...'

'And fish!'

'And there are woods all around and George, you'll simply love it!'

'Me?' said George, in what Milly called his choky voice. 'You mean I'm to go too?'

The children both laughed delightedly. 'Why, *of*

course,' they said together. 'Do you suppose,' Milly added, 'that we'd go off and leave you?'

'Well,' George said slowly, 'I hadn't planned on taking a . . . what do you call it . . . *holiday* but this that you've told me does sound attractive . . . *most* attractive.'

Milly and Tommy went on to add more details. They always rode in the back seat on the way, and George could sit between them. They stopped for lunch at the same place every year, such a nice restaurant at the edge of a wood where there was a parrot.

'He can talk, but nothing like you, George,' Tommy said.

They always stayed overnight at a place called a *motel,* but after much discussion it was decided now that George would be more comfortable just to sleep in the station wagon.

Mrs Weaver had to call more than once that evening before the children realized it was time for bed, so busy had they been telling George all about the delights of the holiday.

Every night after this they all sat under the apple tree and talked and talked. The trip itself, the cabin, the lake, the woods, the fish Father caught and Mother cooked on the big outdoor oven, the bonfire they had on cool nights when they all sat around the blazing logs, singing to Father's guitar which Mother always brought down from the attic before they left home and put in the station wagon . . . all this the children recounted while George listened, his ears quivering with eagerness.

'You are pleased about going, aren't you, George?' Milly asked once.

'I may say,' George stated very slowly, 'that I have never been as pleased over anything in all my life.'

One afternoon the family excitement rose to fever pitch. A beautiful new little motorboat was hauled along the drive and left in the garden! It was a great surprise from Father, and nobody could think or talk of anything else all evening. The boat would ride on top of the station wagon as they went to Canada.

'We have an old one up there but nothing like as

pretty as this one,' Milly said when they were under the apple tree. 'Besides, the other motor was always stopping and leaving us sitting out in the middle of the lake while Father tinkered with it. Now we'll just go putt-putting along. George, can you swim?' she added suddenly.

'Well, as a matter of fact, I can't', George admitted. 'At least I'd rather not try. My grandfather always said that we rabbits and hares were much better to stick to the land. And I always have.'

'Oh, then you can't go in the boat! Father has a rule

that no one who can't swim can go out on the water. Will you mind very much?'

'Not a bit,' George said cheerfully. 'I'll have plenty to occupy me in the woods. I think *for various reasons* I'll spend most of my time there.'

The days passed, though the children thought, very slowly, but at last it was Monday with Wednesday morning the day they would leave. Suitcases were being packed and boxes stood about in the kitchen. Milly's best doll was ready in a basket and Tommy's balls were in a special bag. George found his ears standing straight up with the thrill of it all. The dinner conversation was very interesting and agreeable that evening, he thought, until suddenly Milly spoke.

'Oh, I can hardly wait! George is going to sit between Tommy and me on the back seat.'

'What was that you said?' their father asked quickly.

'Why . . . why,' Milly stammered, 'I just said George would sit with us going up. He won't be the least bit of trouble, Father. We've talked it all over with him.'

'Now listen!' Mr Weaver said very seriously. 'There is something *I want* to talk over with you and Tommy. All this business of *George* has to stop. It's all right for very little children to imagine things, but for a big girl and boy such as you two are to keep pretending there is a rabbit here who holds conversations with you and who *wears glasses* – well, that is ridiculous and not good for you. I'm putting an end to it right now in this way. George, whatever he is, is *not* going to Canada!'

'But Father,' Milly cried in a heartbroken voice, 'we've promised him and he's looking forward to it so!'

'There,' Mr Weaver said almost violently, 'that's just what I mean. This thing has gone too far. We'll all be losing our wits pretty soon. I don't want either of you to speak of George again!'

Then there was a great silence in the dining room while George crouched down behind the drier with his

nose in his paws and quivered all over. He tried hard to control himself but he still trembled. He heard the children excuse themselves, push back their chairs and evidently leave the table. Then after a little while Mr Weaver spoke, apparently to Mrs Weaver.

'Well,' he said, 'something had to be done, and that was the best way to do it. Why are you looking at me that way?'

'Because,' said Mrs Weaver slowly, 'I think you've just spoiled a very beautiful thing.'

And then there was quiet again.

That evening under the apple tree Milly cried and Tommy cried and while George didn't actually cry his voice was very *choky* indeed.

'Now we won't have nearly as good a time,' Milly moaned. 'But it's not us I'm thinking of most. It's you, George. You *are* terribly disappointed, aren't you?'

'Well,' said George, speaking very carefully, 'I must admit I ... I was *anticipating* the ... ah ... trip. But

my grandfather always said, "If you can't have something you want, forget it!" I'll try to do that.'

'And I thought maybe you could sleep with me in my bunk,' Tommy said sadly, not even asking what *anticipate* meant. 'It's chilly up there and you're so warm to cuddle up to. Oh, dear!'

It was a sad evening.

Even the next day the house was quieter, with less shouting and laughter and calling back and forth than there had been before. In the late afternoon the children went with their mother as usual to the station. When they returned they all came in the back door and all at the same time saw the piece of paper propped up against the sugar bowl on the kitchen table. Mr Weaver read it aloud while the others looked on.

> I HAV gone But enjoiEd
> MY ViSIT. LuV to ALL
>
> George
>
> P.S. my grandFather DIDNT
> TEeCH SpELINg.
>
> G.

'Well, well,' Mr Weaver laughed. 'Very clever! Who did this?'

But nobody spoke a word. Milly ran suddenly to the counter and reached in behind the breadbox. She drew something out and gave a cry.

'He's left them! He's left his glasses!' she said, and then held them out to Mr Weaver. 'Oh Father, surely you'll believe in him now!'

Mr Weaver slowly took the tiny spectacles in his hands and stared at them with his mouth open. It was his turn to be silent.

The children came close to their mother, their voices raised in distress.

'Mother, Mother, you do think he'll come back sometime, don't you?'

Mrs Weaver glanced at her husband who still stood fingering the little glasses, with the strange expression on his face. Her eyes looked past him, far away, as though she was remembering something.

Then she smiled. The very smile the children loved best of all. It was the one that showed how much she loved them and how completely she understood all they were thinking.

'Yes,' she said softly, drawing them to her, 'I'm sure George will come back to you. Often.'

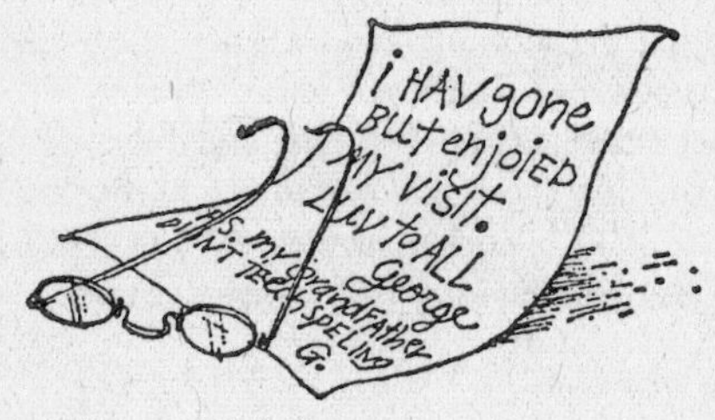

ABOUT THE AUTHOR

Agnes Sligh Turnbull was born in New Alexandria, Pennsylvania, a small village about 30 miles east of Pittsburgh, and spent her childhood in the horse-and-buggy days. She recalls sleigh-rides in winter, drives around the countryside in summer, picnics, lawn-parties, and in general slow days of calm and sunny years. After leaving the village school she went to a boarding school, then a Teacher's College, and finally the University of Chicago. She taught English in various high schools until she married in 1918. She has a daughter and four grandchildren.

Mrs Sligh Turnbull's first story was published in 1920, and for some years she produced mainly short stories; her first novel, *The Rolling Years*, appeared in 1936. When questioned on her method of writing, she says she works only during the morning and in pencil – she doesn't even own a typewriter. She loves music, theatre, cinema, gardening and bridge, and says if she could live her life again with her family she would like to live in the country with a horse, a collie, a cocker spaniel and a row of bee-boxes, such as her grandmother had, along the garden wall.

If you have enjoyed this book and would like to know about others which we publish, why not join the Puffin Club? You will receive the club magazine, *Puffin Post,* four times a year and a smart badge and membership book. You will also be able to enter all the competitions. For details, send a stamped addressed envelope to:

The Puffin Club Dept. A
Penguin Books Limited
Bath Road
Harmondsworth
Middlesex